Bear

A Force of Nature
Reflection • Strength • Healing

DayDreams Studio Press

"Totem Within Series"

This Book Belongs To:

_____

_____

Welcome,
Seeker of Stillness

You Are A Force of Nature

❖

You hold in your hands
more than a journal—you
hold a sacred space for
reflection.
Like the bear entering
hibernation, you are
invited to pause, turn
inward, and discover the
strength that comes from
stillness.

The Power of the Bear

The bear is seen as a symbol of introspection and renewal, guiding those it chooses toward finding strength in stillness and wisdom in solitude.

It encourages taking time to rest, reflect, and heal, much like the bear's winter hibernation.

This powerful creature also signifies the importance of grounding yourself and protecting your sacred space before emerging transformed.

The Bear Symbolizes:

Reflection -
The courage to pause and look within

Strength -
A Power that comes from being grounded

Healing -
The ability to rest, restore, and renew

Wisdom -
Understanding gained through stillness

Renewal -
Emerging stronger from reflection

As you write in this journal, embrace these
qualities...

This is YOUR sacred space.
There are no rules, only invitations.

You are braver than you believe, stronger than you seem, and smarter than you think."
—Christopher Robin, Pooh's Grand Adventure

_____

_____

_____

_____

_____

_____

_____

_____

_____

_____

_____

To doubt everything, or, to believe everything,
are two equally convenient solutions;
both dispense with the necessity of reflection.
—Henri Poincaré

_____

_____

_____

_____

_____

_____

_____

_____

_____

_____

Only one who devotes himself to a cause with his
whole strength and soul can be a true master.
For this reason mastery demands all of a person.
—Albert Einstein

_____

_____

_____

_____

_____

_____

_____

_____

_____

_____

Healing is a matter of time, but it is sometimes
also a matter of opportunity.
— Hippocrates.

_____

_____

_____

_____

_____

_____

_____

_____

_____

_____

In the depth of winter I finally learned that
there was in me an invincible summer.
—Albert Camus

_____

_____

_____

_____

_____

_____

_____

_____

_____

_____

_____

_____

Over every mountain there is a path, although it
may not be seen from the valley.
—Theodore Roethke

_____

_____

_____

_____

_____

_____

_____

_____

_____

_____

_____

_____

"We do not learn from experience... we learn from reflecting on experience." — John Dewey

_____

_____

_____

_____

_____

_____

_____

_____

_____

_____

_____

_____

_____

_____

_____

_____

_____

_____

_____

_____

_____

_____

_____

Stop to Discover *Ikigai* The Joy of a Meaningful Life
Explore the intersection of your passions, skills, and
purpose—much like a personal totem—to lead a more
fulfilling life. This alignment will assist you in establishing
goals that promote both personal and professional
growth.

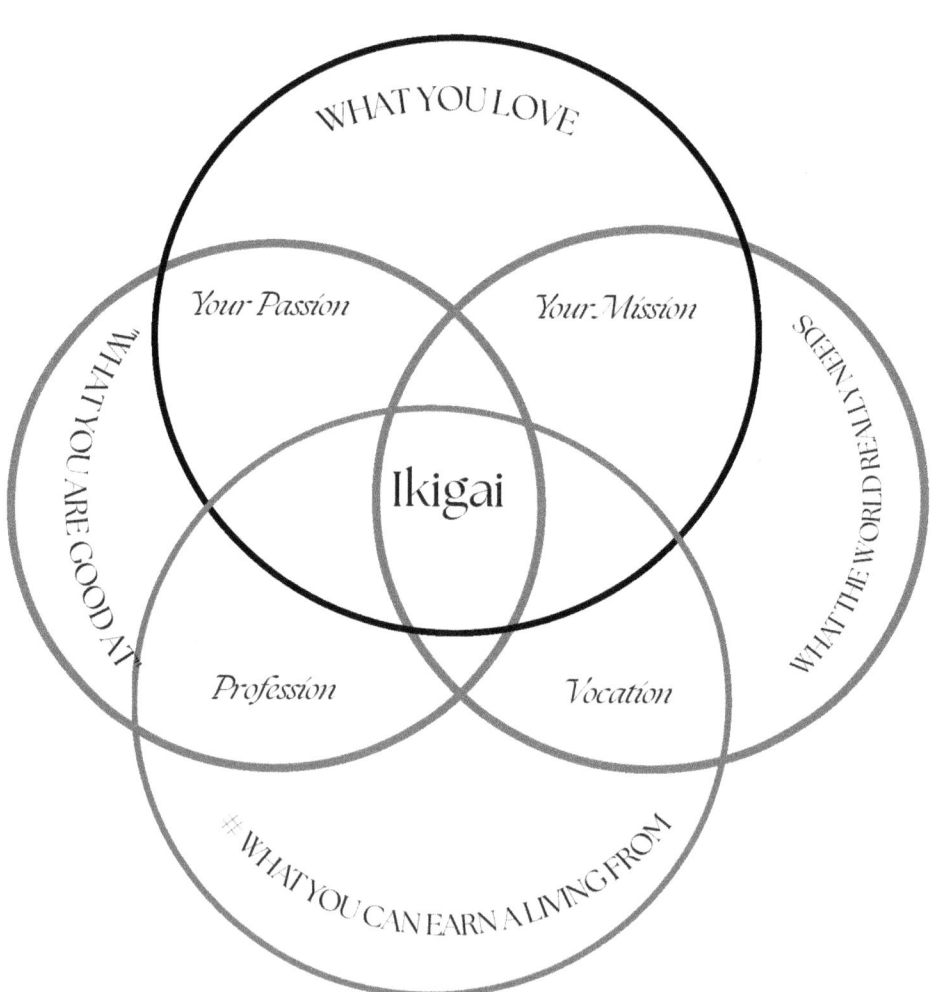

"Knowing yourself is the beginning of all wisdom." — Aristotle

---

"Remember what you loved to do and who you were before the world told you who to be. " — JHS

"Your visions will become clear only when you can look into your own heart. Who looks outside, dreams; who looks inside, awakes."— Carl Jung

_____

_____

_____

_____

_____

_____

_____

_____

_____

_____

_____

_____

"In the midst of movement and chaos, keep stillness inside of you."— Deepak Chopra

_____

_____

_____

_____

_____

_____

_____

_____

_____

_____

_____

_____

"We cannot solve our problems with the same thinking we used when we created them."
— Albert Einstein

_____

_____

_____

_____

_____

_____

_____

_____

_____

_____

_____

"The cave you fear to enter holds the treasure you seek."
— Joseph Campbell

"To be born again is not to become somebody else, but to become ourselves."
— Thomas Merton

"In the depth of winter, the bear knows:
rest is not weakness, it is wisdom."
— Unknown

_____

_____

_____

_____

_____

_____

_____

_____

_____

_____

_____

"The bear teaches us that true power comes from knowing when to pause, rest, and emerge renewed."— Native American Wisdom

_____

_____

_____

_____

_____

_____

_____

_____

_____

_____

_____

_____

_____

Final Thought

This journal represents
your dedication to
personal growth.

As you revisit these
pages, take a moment to
reflect on your journey
—observe how much you
have accomplished.

"As you continue your
journey, may the bear's
wisdom deepen within
you with each passing
season."

May you have a beautiful life

Uncover your next totem animal!
Subscribe for updates, and enter for a
chance to win a complimentary journal at
https://joannesullam.com